STRATEGIES
FOR TEACHING
Middle-Level
General Music

MENC wishes to thank
Carolynn A. Lindeman for developing and coordinating this series;
June M. Hinckley and *Suzanne M. Shull*
for selecting, writing, and editing the strategies for this book;
and the following teachers for submitting strategies:

Robert Amchin

Patricia L. Arnett

Stephan P. Barnicle

Charles Baugh

J. Bryan Burton

Marilyn Davidson

Jo-Ann Decker-St. Pierre

Ed Duling

Lawrence Eisman

Martha Giles

Darla S. Hanley

Pamela Hopton-Jones

Kirk Kassner

Gloria J. Kiester

Patrice Madura

Patty A. Perec

Judith Teicher

Kathleen R. Vande Berg

Valerie Vander Mark

Roberta Volkmann

Fred Wein

Jackie Wiggins

YOUR KEY TO
IMPLEMENTING
THE NATIONAL
STANDARDS
FOR MUSIC
EDUCATION

STRATEGIES FOR TEACHING

Middle-Level General Music

The National Association for Music Education

COMPILED
AND EDITED
BY
June M. Hinckley
and
Suzanne M. Shull

Published in partnership with Music Educators National Conference
1806 Robert Fulton Drive, Reston, Virginia 20191-4348

Published by Rowman & Littlefield Education
A division of Rowman & Littlefield Publishers, Inc.
A wholly owned subsidiary of The Rowman & Littlefield Publishing Group, Inc.
4501 Forbes Boulevard, Suite 200, Lanham, Maryland 20706
http://www.rowmaneducation.com

Estover Road, Plymouth PL6 7PY, United Kingdom

British Library Cataloguing in Publication Information Available

Library of Congress Cataloging-in-Publication Data Available

ISBN: 1-56545-084-1

♾™ The paper used in this publication meets the minimum requirements of American National Standard for Information Sciences—Permanence of Paper for Printed Library Materials, ANSI/NISO Z39.48-1992.

Printed in the United States of America

CONTENTS

PREFACE

The Music Educators National Conference (MENC) created the *Strategies for Teaching* series to help preservice and in-service music educators implement the K–12 National Standards for Music Education and the MENC Prekindergarten Standards. To address the many components of the school music curriculum, each book in the series focuses on a specific curricular area and a particular level. The result is eleven books spanning the K–12 areas of band, chorus, general music, strings/orchestra, guitar, keyboard, and specialized ensembles. A prekindergarten book and a guide for college music methods classes complete the series.

The purpose of the series is to seize the opportunity presented by the landmark education legislation of 1994. With the passage of the Goals 2000: Educate America Act, the arts were established for the first time in our country's history as a core, challenging subject in which all students need to demonstrate competence. Voluntary academic standards were called for in all nine of the identified core subjects—standards specifying what students need to know and be able to do when they exit grades 4, 8, and 12.

In music, content and achievement standards were drafted by an MENC task force. They were examined and commented on by music teachers across the country, and the task force reviewed their comments and refined the standards. While all students in grades K–8 are expected to meet the achievement standards specified for those levels, two levels of achievement—proficient and advanced—are designated for students in grades 9–12. Students who elect music courses for one to two years beyond grade 8 are expected to perform at the proficient level. Students who elect music courses for three to four years beyond grade 8 are expected to perform at the advanced level.

The music standards, together with the dance, theatre, and visual arts standards, were presented in final form—*National Standards for Arts Education*—to the U.S. Secretary of Education in March 1994. Recognizing the importance of early childhood education, MENC went beyond the K–12 standards and established content and achievement standards for the prekindergarten level as well, which are included in MENC's *The School Music Program: A New Vision*.

Now the challenge at hand is to implement the standards at the state and local levels. Implementation may require schools to expand the resources necessary to achieve the standards as specified in MENC's *Opportunity-to-Learn Standards for Music Instruction: Grades PreK–12.* Teachers will need to examine their curricula to determine if they lead to achievement of the standards. For many, the standards reflect exactly what has always been included in the school music curriculum—they represent best practice. For others, the standards may call for some curricular expansion.

To assist in the implementation process, this series offers teaching strategies illustrating how the music standards can be put into action in the music classroom. The strategies themselves do not suggest a curriculum. That, of course, is the responsibility of school districts and individual teachers. The strategies, however, are designed to help in curriculum development, lesson planning, and assessment of music learning.

The teaching strategies are based on the content and achievement standards specified in the *National Standards for Arts Education* (K–12) and *The School Music Program: A New Vision* (PreK–12). Although the strategies, like the standards, are designed primarily for four-year-olds, fourth graders, eighth graders, and high school seniors, many may be developmentally appropriate for students in other grades. Each strategy, a lesson appropriate for a portion of a class session or a complete class session, includes an objective (a clear statement of what the student will be able to do), a list of necessary materials, a description of what prior student learning and experiences are expected, a set of procedures, and the indicators of success. A follow-up section identifies ways learning may be expanded.

The *Guide for Music Methods Classes* contains strategies appropriate for preservice instructional settings in choral, instrumental, and general music methods classes. The teaching strategies in this guide relate to the other books in the series and reflect a variety of teaching/learning styles.

Bringing a series of thirteen books from vision to reality in a little over a year's time required tremendous commitment from many, many music educators—not to mention the tireless help of the MENC publications staff. Literally hundreds of music teachers across the country answered the call to participate in this project, the largest such participation in an MENC publishing endeavor. The contributions of these teachers and the books' editors are proudly presented in the various publications.

—*Carolynn A. Lindeman*
Series Editor

*Carolynn A. Lindeman, professor of music at San Francisco State University and president of the Music Educators National Conference (1996–98), served on the MENC task force that developed the music education standards. She is the author of three college textbooks (*The Musical Classroom, PianoLab, *and* MusicLab) *and numerous articles.*

INTRODUCTION

General music teachers at the middle level provide the all-important bridge between required general music instruction for all elementary students and traditionally elective music study for high school students. The National Standards for Music Education do not suggest a significant change in the types of instructional activities teachers offer in middle-level general music, but they provide teachers and administrators with a common, comprehensive vision of music education in today's world. In other words, they give music educators a vehicle with which to "play off the same sheet of music" when planning a sequential music curriculum.

Even before the development of the National Standards, students in many middle-level general music classes were demonstrating the skills and knowledge specified in most of the achievement standards. Because each teacher does not yet focus on *all* of the standards, however, significant differences in student learning still exist in the music classrooms across the country. Now, the strategies in this publication provide middle-level teachers and curriculum planners with a tool for ensuring that a complete program of study, a sequential curriculum, and varied classroom experiences are offered to all music students.

These strategies are based on the suggestions of many teachers and have been successfully used by music teachers in various learning environments. The approaches suggested require materials that can be easily located. As often as possible, textbooks and recordings produced by national publishers are suggested, and publishers of the materials are given within the lessons and in the Resources section of this book. The newest versions as well as older editions of these texts are full of wonderful ideas and materials that can be adapted to extend or reinforce the strategies included here.

The strategies employ a variety of literature—from operas and traditional Western music to Native American songs, Japanese music, and blues. They reflect the changing multiethnic nature of America and recognize the importance new technologies play in the learning environment. The strategies also include conventional and time-honored music-making traditions. Teachers should, of course, adjust these strategies to meet the needs of their particular students and the local community. Making the general music class relevant to students' varying interests and abilities helps ensure that students will apply and retain the skills and knowledge on which the strategies focus.

Although each teaching strategy in this publication addresses one achievement standard, more than one standard can and probably should be addressed within the same lesson. For instance, when learning about composition, students must employ skills in notating music. Making connections with other curricular areas may also involve teaching historical or cultural contexts. Students can perform their own compositions, and the suggested activities for singing can be repeated and reinforced by having students play instruments. Students can evaluate their own compositions and performances as well as those of their friends. Especially in schools where contact time with students is limited, merging the lessons to accommodate teaching more than one achievement standard is encouraged.

Since assessing and evaluating students is an important part of instruction, indicators of success, or assessment models, are included in each strategy. Such assessment informs the teacher, as well as the students, about where the students are in the process of acquiring the skills and knowledge central to the strategy. The indicators suggested here are designed to be done at the end of the particular strategy, but they can also be incorporated throughout the lesson to take the pulse of how well the students are learning.

Many of the suggested indicators employ teacher and student observation based on evaluative criteria on which both have agreed as a part of the lesson. This type of assessment or evaluation lends itself to the creation of portfolios—purposeful collections of work and observations that serve as a long-term record of each student's accomplishments and progress. Both the teacher and the student take responsibility for what is included in the portfolio and for evaluating it.

Finally, the subtitle to the *National Standards for Arts Education,* "What Every Student Should Know and Be Able to Do in the Arts," is a concept that should be taken very seriously. Simply making music without knowing about it does not engage students in the reflective, evaluative cognition that is so important to long-term retention of knowledge. On the other hand, simply learning about music and never experiencing the refinement that occurs during rehearsals, the concentration inherent in making beautiful music, the cooperation needed to create an ensemble effort, and the final joy of performance leaves out a vital element of the music experience.

All of the achievement standards have an essential place in the middle-level general music classroom. Together, the standards and the strategies in this book can serve as a blueprint, or guide, in helping to achieve a balance among performance, evaluative, creative, and integrated activities in middle-level general music classes.

STRATEGIES

STANDARD 1A

Singing, alone and with others, a varied repertoire of music: Students sing accurately and with good breath control throughout their singing ranges, alone and in small and large ensembles.

Objective

■ Students will sing all phrases of a song with good breath control and with accurate pitch and rhythm.

Materials

■ "Over My Head," in *Share the Music,* Grade 5 (New York: Macmillan/McGraw-Hill, 1995), or any song demanding relatively long, sustained phrases, such as "Follow the Drinkin' Gourd," in *The Music Connection,* Grade 3 (Parsippany, NJ: Silver Burdett Ginn, 1995), *Share the Music,* Grade 6, or *Music and You,* Grades 5 and 8 (New York: Macmillan/McGraw-Hill, 1991); "Scarborough Fair," in *The Music Connection,* Grade 6, *Share the Music,* Grade 6, *Music and You,* Grade 6, or *World of Music,* Grade 6 (Parsippany, NJ: Silver Burdett Ginn, 1991); or "Shenandoah," in *The Music Connection,* Grade 8, *Share the Music,* Grade 6, *Music and You,* Grade 5, or *World of Music,* Grade 8

■ Audiocassette recorder with microphone and blank tape (optional)

Procedures

1. Have students sing the song once through and evaluate their ability to sing each phrase in one breath. (If possible, record their singing of the song.) Tell them that they are going to have an opportunity to improve their singing of the song by concentrating on breath control.

2. Ask students to stand with shoulders down and heads straight, with hands on their lower ribs. Have them bend over and pant to feel the muscles that support breathing. (With this age group, it may be best to avoid using the word "diaphragm.") Explain that those muscles control inhaling and exhaling and that breathing for singing needs to be much deeper than for speaking in order to support the singing tone. Have students stand straight and, while lightly touching their lower ribs with their hands, inhale silently and without moving; to a count of five, ask them to relax their throats so that they feel a space in the back of the mouth, almost as if yawning. Then, ask them to inhale as if sipping juice through a straw and filling an inner tube around the waist.

3. Have students sing the song again, taking the time before each phrase for the deep breath described above, as you count to four. Repeat the song, asking students to take in just as much air before each phrase but to only a count of two.

4. Have students sing the song one more time. This time, ask them to breathe in for just one count. Have them reevaluate their ability to sing the long phrases well, now that they are breathing deeply and correctly controlling their breath during each phrase. If necessary, repeat the above steps.

5. Ask students to sing the song again, having them raise a hand each time they take a breath so that you can assess whether they are able to sing each phrase in one breath.

6. Have the class establish criteria for judging an accurate performance of the song (that is, with correct pitches and rhythms). Then, have students practice the song in small (3–5) groups, working for pitch and rhythm accuracy, as well as for good breath control. Within these groups, have students make suggestions for improvement of their singing.

(continued)

Prior Knowledge and Experiences

- Students have been introduced to basic concepts of correct breathing, posture, and diction.

- Students have sung a variety of songs and have had frequent experience singing in small groups for the rest of the class.

- Students know by memory the words and music for the song to be used in the lesson.

7. Ask students to sing the song all together once more and to evaluate their performance. (If possible, record their singing and have them compare it to a recording of their singing of the song at the beginning of class.)

Indicators of Success

- Students identify their ability to sing long phrases well and recognize the value of deep breathing and breath control.

- Students increase their ability to sing the song with accurate pitch and rhythm and positively assess their performance.

Follow-up

- Have volunteers briefly recount their experience in the class and how they feel that correct breathing helped them sing the song better.

- Have students apply the principles emphasized in this lesson to singing other songs. Emphasize the importance of well-formed vowel sound in increasing pitch accuracy and blend in group singing.

STANDARD 1B

Singing, alone and with others, a varied repertoire of music: Students sing with expression and technical accuracy a repertoire of vocal literature with a level of difficulty of 2, on a scale of 1 to 6, including some songs performed from memory.

Objective

- Students will perform selected choral literature with expression, with rhythmic and melodic accuracy, and from memory.

Materials

- Two- and three-part octavo selections

- Choral music from textbook series, such as "Springtime" ("La Primavera"), in *The Music Connection,* Grade 6 (Parsippany, NJ: Silver Burdett Ginn, 1995), or *World of Music,* Grade 6 (Parsippany, NJ: Silver Burdett Ginn, 1991); or "Earth Day Every Day," in *Share the Music,* Grade 6 (New York: Macmillan/McGraw-Hill, 1995)

- Audiocassette recorder with microphone and blank tape

Prior Knowledge and Experiences

- Students have learned the words and notes of the selected songs.

Procedures

1. Discuss with students how the songs they have been learning will contribute to the school's celebration of Earth Day. Explain how understanding the meaning of the songs can contribute to expressive singing. Review the lyrics of the selected songs and discuss their meaning.

2. Have students make an audio recording of their singing of the selections. Then have them listen to the tape and discuss whether they are singing the music accurately and conveying the expression and meaning appropriately. Lead them to discover any inaccuracies in pitch and rhythm.

3. Review the meaning of the dynamics and other expressive markings in each selection. Have students discuss whether they have observed these markings in their singing and how attention to them can help in interpreting the songs for their audience.

4. Ask students whether they think their diction is precise and how they could improve it.

5. As students discover ways to improve their performance, have them rehearse the songs with attention to their discoveries. Challenge the students to sing the songs from memory.

Indicators of Success

- Students sing selected choral literature with expression and accuracy, with some selections performed from memory.

- Students identify inaccuracies in their performance and work to correct them.

Follow-up

- Have students listen to a recording made of their performance at the Earth Day celebration and compare it to their earlier recording. Ask them to identify the ways in which their technical accuracy and interpretation of the music has improved.

Singing, alone and with others, a varied repertoire of music: Students sing music representing diverse genres and cultures, with expression appropriate for the work being performed.

Objective

- Students will sing the melody of a South African freedom song with appropriate expressive qualities.

Materials

- "Siyahamba," with accompanying CD, in *The Music Connection,* Grade 6 (Parsippany: Silver Burdett Ginn, 1995), or *Share the Music,* Grade 6 (New York: Macmillan/McGraw-Hill, 1995)
- CD player

Prior Knowledge and Experiences

- Students have studied African musical culture.

Procedures

1. Introduce "Siyahamba" by explaining that it is a South African freedom song. Discuss the text, asking students questions such as "Are there any hidden meanings?" (Explain how slaves used "signal songs" in the United States in the escape to freedom through the Underground Railroad. Codes were used so that information could be communicated about routes for escapes, meeting plans, and important news such as danger during escapes. This transmission of information links signal songs with African "news songs.") Ask what languages are used. (English and Zulu)

2. Play the recording of "Siyahamba" and ask students to listen closely to the melody, the text, and the singing style.

3. Lead the class in a discussion of the meaning of the song, including how the musical elements, such as syncopation, support the text. Then ask whether any of them can sing a phrase of the song (in English, in Zulu, or on neutral syllables). Have students try singing phrases in the style that they heard on the recording.

4. Once students can sing some of the phrases, have them learn the rest of the melody by reading the notation. Encourage students to identify the musical structure of "Siyahamba." (Verse-refrain)

5. Discuss with the students the role of music in the South African freedom movement. Explain that in their struggle for freedom, many South African blacks have identified with African Americans who have faced racial discrimination. Some elements of the music of the South African freedom movement are similar to music of African American hymns and spirituals.

6. Based on what students have learned about the text's meaning, have them sing with particular attention to expressive qualities.

Indicators of Success

- Students sing "Siyahamba" expressively and with technical accuracy.

Follow-up

- Have students learn harmony parts to "Siyahamba" so that their performance will be more within the style of group singing, which is the appropriate style for this song.

Singing, alone and with others, a varied repertoire of music: Students sing music representing diverse genres and cultures, with expression appropriate for the work being performed.

Objective

- Students will sing a Japanese folk song accurately and expressively.

Materials

- "Sakura," with accompanying recording, in *The Music Connection,* Grades 4 and 7 (Parsippany, NJ: Silver Burdett Ginn, 1995); *Share the Music,* Grade 3 (New York: Macmillan/McGraw-Hill, 1995); *Music and You,* Grade 4 (New York: Macmillan/ McGraw-Hill, 1991); or *World of Music,* Grades 4 and 7 (Parsippany, NJ: Silver Burdett Ginn, 1991)

- Instrumental recording of "Sakura" (for example, in excerpt from *Japanese Masterpieces for the Koto,* on accompanying CD for *The Music Connection,* Grade 4

- Multiple copies of evaluation form for each student (see accompanying figure)

- Audio-playback equipment

Procedures

1. Have students listen to vocal and instrumental recordings of "Sakura." Ask them to explain in musical terms how the song exemplifies the axiom of "maximum effect from minimum material" (for example, pentatonic melody, simple accompaniment).

2. Rehearse the song in the large-group setting. Then divide class into small groups. Have each group prepare an a capella performance of the song for their peers.

3. Invite groups to sing for each other. While each group performs, have the other groups listen and then complete an evaluation form, discussing the merits of each performance. Collect the evaluation forms after each performance.

4. Distribute completed evaluation forms to the appropriate groups. Have each group consider how it can improve its performance based on the evaluations and then continue to practice the song.

5. Finally, have each group perform again for the class, keeping in mind the previous evaluations.

Indicators of Success

- Students sing "Sakura" accurately and expressively.

Follow-up

- Have groups of students list their thoughts about the meaning of "Sakura." Consider having a student narrator or emcee read some of these thoughts during a public performance of the song.

- Have students write haiku verses and set them to music using the same pentatonic scale as the one used in "Sakura." To ensure success, consider having students use pitched percussion instruments or keyboards.

(continued)

Prior Knowledge and Experiences

- Students have studied the effect of the basic axiom of Japanese art: "maximum effect from minimum material."

- Students can sing with attention to accurate pitches and rhythm, good breath support, and appropriate expression and style.

- Students have prepared a form for evaluating their singing (see accompanying figure).

Name of Singer	Accuracy	Style/ Expression	Tone Quality	Breathing	Posture/ Presence
Score (circle)	1 2 3 4 5	1 2 3 4 5	1 2 3 4 5	1 2 3 4 5	1 2 3 4 5
Explanation of Score					

Evaluation Form. (Note: *1=highest level of performance; 5=lowest level of performance.*)

STANDARD 1D

Singing, alone and with others, a varied repertoire of music:
Students sing music written in two and three parts.

Objective

- From nonstandard notation, students will sing a song with three harmony parts.

Materials

- "Rock-a My Soul," in *The Music Connection,* Grades 6 and 8 (Parsippany, NJ: Silver Burdett Ginn, 1995); *Music and You,* Grade 6 (New York: Macmillan/McGraw-Hill, 1991); or *World of Music,* Grades 6 and 8 (Parsippany, NJ: Silver Burdett Ginn, 1991)

- Three harmony parts for "Rock-a My Soul" (see page 14)

Prior Knowledge and Experience

- Students can sing canons and songs with ostinatos.

- Students have sung music written in two or three parts.

Procedures

1. Introduce the song "Rock-a My Soul" by having all students sing the melody from their music book.

2. Have students learn Part I. Explain to students that Part I begins on *do* of the key, and that when the text drops below or rises above the line, they should adjust the pitch in that direction by a step or half step (see syllable names in parentheses). If students are familiar with solfège, have them sing the syllables before using words.

3. Divide class in half and have one half sing the melody while the other half sings Part I. Encourage students with changing voices to sing in the octave that is comfortable for them.

4. Repeat steps 2 and 3 with Part II, then Part III.

5. Put all of the parts together, dividing the students into parts according to which part is in the most comfortable range for each student's particular voice. Put the piece together with the melody and all three harmony parts. (If the class has not had experience singing in three parts, first have them sing only two of the harmony parts with the melody.)

6. Encourage solo or group volunteers to take turns singing the melody to the chordal accompaniment of their classmates.

Indicators of Success

- Reading from nonstandard notation, students successfully perform three harmony parts with the melody of "Rock-a My Soul."

Follow-up

- Have students use chordal harmony to arrange a favorite ballad. Then have the class sing the chordal harmony as soloists sing the melody.

(continued)

Rock-a My Soul

Arr. P. Hopton-Jones

Part I (*do*)

C		G7		F	G7
				(*re*) Abra-	

~~(*do*) Rock-a my soul in the bosom of Abraham,~~ _____

(*ti*) Rock-a my soul in the bosom of   (*ti*) ham,

C		G7	C

~~(*do*) Rock-a my soul in the bosom of Abraham,~~ _____ ~~(*do*) soul.~~ _____

(*ti*) Oh, Rock-a my

Part II (*mi*)

C		G7		F	G7
				(*fa*) Abra-	

~~(*mi*) Rock-a my soul in the bosom of Abraham,~~

(*re*) Rock-a my soul in the bosom of   (*re*) ham,

C		G7	C

~~(*mi*) Rock-a my soul in the bosom of Abraham,~~ _____ ~~(*mi*) soul.~~ _____

(*re*) Oh, Rock-a my

Part III (*sol*)

C		G7		F	G7
				(*la*) Abra-	

~~(*sol*) Rock-a my soul in the bosom of Abraham,~~ _____

(*fa*) Rock-a my soul in the bosom of   (*fa*) ham,

C		G7	C

~~(*sol*) Rock-a my soul in the bosom of Abraham,~~ _____ ~~(*sol*) soul.~~ _____

(*fa*) Oh, Rock-a my

STANDARD 2A

Performing on instruments, alone and with others, a varied repertoire of music: Students perform on at least one instrument accurately and independently, alone and in small and large ensembles, with good posture, good playing position, and good breath, bow, or stick control.

Objective

■ Students will perform with proper technique on the soprano recorder a piece that uses the notes B, A, and G.

Materials

■ Soprano recorders

■ Notation for a song using the notes B, A, and G, such as "Old Ark's A-Moverin'," in *Share the Music: Playing the Recorder*, Grade 6 (New York: Macmillan/McGraw-Hill, 1995)

■ Chalkboard or blank transparency (see step 6)

■ Overhead projector, if transparency is used

Prior Knowledge and Experiences

■ Students have listened to a recording of recorder music or to their teacher modeling correct playing technique, but they have not played the recorder before.

Procedures

1. Taking the words from a simple poem or rhyme, have students create a simple song using the notes B, A, and G. On the chalkboard or on a transparency, write "B," "A," or "G" over the words or syllables of the poem to create a tune (see the following figure, for example). Have students sing the song in rhythm using the letter names. Suggest that students give their song a title.

G G B B   G G   B   G G B B   B A G

When in dan-ger, When in doubt, Run in cir - cles, scream and shout.

"When in Danger," melody by R. Amchin.

2. On your recorder, show students where to place fingers for each note (B, A, and G). Have students practice each note by using their fingers on their desks (one finger down for B, two for A, and three for G).

3. Demonstrate potential problems and solutions for beginning players; for example, proper breath control and covering finger holes completely.

4. Distribute recorders to students and have them play B, A, and G, working for a clear tone.

5. Have students echo patterns from the created song as you either play the patterns or sing them while demonstrating correct fingering. For example, play "G, G, B, B" and have students echo that pattern. Gradually begin to play longer phrases until students can play the whole song.

6. On the chalkboard or on a transparency, show students the notation for B, A, and G on the staff. Have students write the notation for the created song and then play the song from their notation.

7. Using notation, introduce another three-note song, such as "Old Ark's A-Moverin'."

(continued)

Indicators of Success

- Demonstrating good posture and playing position, students accurately play songs using B, A, and G on the recorder.

Follow-up

- Have students individually create songs using the three notes they have learned and play their songs for the class. Have them teach their songs to the other students in the class by echo playing.
- Teach the students more notes on the recorder, having students sing the notes first, play the notes, and then read them.

Performing on instruments, alone and with others, a varied repertoire of music: Students perform music representing diverse genres and cultures, with expression appropriate for the work being performed.

Objective

- Students will perform an accompaniment to a Yoruban song with rhythmic and stylistic accuracy on selected African percussion instruments.

Materials

- "Three Yoruba Native Songs of Nigeria," arr. Henry Leck and Prince Julius Adeniyi (Ft. Lauderdale, FL: Plymouth Music Company, 1994)
- Cowbell or double bell
- Small talking drum, large talking drum, and conga (or classroom instruments of appropriate size)

Prior Knowledge and Experiences

- Students have been introduced to polyrhythms and have learned to sing either "E Oru O" or "Odun De," from "Three Yoruba Native Songs of Nigeria," with appropriate style and expression for these songs of praise.

Procedures

1. Have entire class sing "E Oru O" ("Greeting") or "Odun De" ("New Year Is Here") as a review. Remind students about the function of these songs in Yoruban culture as songs of praise.

2. Review polyrhythms briefly. Since these songs are both in 6/8 meter, ask students how they might combine the following to create rhythmic ostinatos:

Possible answers:

Have students practice clapping, tapping, and snapping each ostinato. Then divide the students into groups, assign an ostinato to each group, and have the groups perform simultaneously to create polyrhythms.

(continued)

3. Using clapping or other body percussion, teach students the percussion accompaniment for the selected song one line at a time.

4. Divide the class into four groups. Demonstrate how each instrument will be used to perform a specific line. For example: line 1, double bell, alternating high and low; line 2, small talking drum high on eighth notes and low on dotted quarter notes; line 3, large talking drum on three pitches; and line 4, conga. Assign specific instruments to each group, and then have each group select one or two students to play the percussion instruments. Rotate the assignment as the activity is repeated so that all students have the opportunity to play.

5. Have students practice for a short time in their groups. Then have the percussion ensemble—members from all four groups—play the polyrhythm pattern several times together. Emphasize the need for rhythmic accuracy.

6. For a complete performance of the selected song, have students who are not playing instruments sing with the percussion accompaniment. Have students discuss the balance between singers and players and determine whether the dynamics should be loud or soft or whether they should vary during the performance.

7. Have students repeat their performance, applying the dynamics and balance they have discussed for an expressive performance.

Indicators of Success

- Students demonstrate accuracy in playing and singing the polyrhythms.

- Students accurately perform the song on percussion instruments to accompany singing.

- Students identify and apply appropriate dynamics for an expressive performance of the selected song.

Follow-up

- Have students improvise or compose new polyrhythmic patterns for the percussion accompaniment.

Performing on instruments, alone and with others, a varied repertoire of music: Students perform music representing diverse genres and cultures, with expression appropriate for the work being performed.

Objective

- Students will play folk songs from different ethnic origins, using stylistically appropriate articulation.

Materials

- "Land of the Silver Birch," in *The Music Connection*, Grades 3 and 4 (Parsippany, NJ: Silver Burdett Ginn, 1995); *Music and You*, Grade 6 (New York: Macmillan/McGraw-Hill, 1991); or *World of Music*, Grade 5 (Parsippany, NJ: Silver Burdett Ginn, 1991)

- "Tumbai" ("Toembaï"), in *Share the Music*, Grade 6 (New York: Macmillan/McGraw-Hill, 1995); or *Music and You*, Grade 6

- "Tzena, Tzena," in *The Music Connection*, Grade 5; *Share the Music*, Grade 5; or *Music and You*, Grade 6

- "The Huron Carol," in *The Music Connection*, Grade 5; *Music and You*, Grade 6; or *World of Music*, Grade 5

- Recorders, keyboards, or other melodic instruments

Procedures

1. Have students play expressively "Tumbai" and "Land of the Silver Birch" on a melodic instrument. Review with students that "Tumbai" is a folk song from Israel and "Land of the Silver Birch" is a Canadian folk song.

2. Ask students which song they played in a more legato manner and which they played in a more percussive fashion. Then ask, "Does the fact that 'Tumbai' is also a folk dance give a clue as to how it should be played?"

3. Have students experiment playing "Tumbai" legato and "Land of the Silver Birch" percussively. Ask them if that seems appropriate. Then have students play "Tumbai" percussively and "Land of the Silver Birch" in a legato style. Discuss with students which style of articulation seems to work best for each piece and why.

4. Review with students the music notation for "Tzena, Tzena" and "The Huron Carol," noting the expressive markings and mood. Explain to the students that these two pieces were composed to be stylistically representative of the same cultures as the two pieces they have been playing.

5. Have students repeat the procedures in step 3, performing "Tzena, Tzena" in a legato style and "The Huron Carol" in a percussive style, and then reversing the styles of articulation. Based on their experience with "Tumbai" and "Land of the Silver Birch," have them identify which song is in the stylistic manner of the Israeli song and which is similar to the Canadian song. Explain that while these songs are stylistically similar, not *all* Canadian or Israeli songs sound the same.

Indicators of Success

- Students successfully perform folk songs in two different styles, using stylistically appropriate articulation.

(continued)

Prior Knowledge and Experiences

- Students can play "Tumbai" and "Land of the Silver Birch" on a melodic instrument.

- Students have sung "Tzena, Tzena" and "The Huron Carol."

Follow-up

- Have students discuss the factors that have influenced the folk music of the Israeli and the Canadian cultures.

- Have students locate and perform with appropriate expression other Israeli and Canadian folk songs.

STANDARD 2D

Performing on instruments, alone and with others, a varied repertoire of music: Students play by ear simple melodies on a melodic instrument and simple accompaniments on a harmonic instrument.

Objective

- Students will play melodies and determine appropriate harmonic accompaniments by ear.

Materials

- Choirchimes, resonator bells, or Orff mallet instruments
- Songs using I, IV, and V chords in the key of C, such as "All Night, All Day," "Let Us Break Bread Together," "We Gather Together," "The First Noel," "Yankee Doodle," "I've Been Working on the Railroad," "Oh, Susanna," "America," "Twinkle, Twinkle, Little Star," "Jingle Bells," "Away in a Manger," and "De colores"
- Song notation (without chords) for the selected songs

Prior Knowledge and Experiences

- Students have had group experience playing chords.

Procedures

1. Review with students which pitches are in the I (C), IV (F), and V (G) chords in the key of C. Assign each student in a small group to play either the root, the third, or the fifth of these chords on choirchimes, resonator bells, or Orff mallet instruments. Then lead the group in playing various progressions of the three chords.

2. For one of the selected songs, have the class establish the starting pitch and sing the song without an accompaniment.

3. Ask the group of students that has the instruments to play the I IV V I chord progression on their instruments as all students listen for the special sound of each chord.

4. Review the song notation and have students identify where certain chords might be included (for example, using the I chord as the final chord or in places where chord tones are obvious). Have students pencil in the possibilities above the melody notation.

5. Have students playing the instruments perform the suggested chords as they sing with the class. Encourage different suggestions and experimentation as they make their decisions "by ear."

6. Follow steps 2–5 with several of the other songs, giving other students the opportunity to play the instruments. Have students identify commonalities in the chord progressions that "work" (for example, each song always ends on the I chord, and the pitches in the melody are often the same as those in the chord).

Indicators of Success

- Students make accurate decisions regarding song accompaniments.
- Students transfer knowledge to increasingly complex songs.
- Students discover that there are patterns to most chord progressions.

Follow-up

- Introduce V7, ii, and vi chords and have students experiment with using them to accompany the songs used in the procedures. Encourage them to discover which chords seem to "work" best.

STANDARD 3A

Improvising melodies, variations, and accompaniments:
Students improvise simple harmonic accompaniments.

Objective

- Students will create counter-melodies on keyboards, choirchimes, resonator bells, or Orff mallet instruments.

Materials

- "All Night, All Day," in *World of Music,* Grade 3 (Parsippany, NJ: Silver Burdett Ginn, 1991), or other lead sheet notation
- Keyboards, choirchimes, resonator bells, or Orff mallet instruments (at least one instrument for each group of students)
- Chalkboard

Prior Knowledge and Experiences

- Students have successfully identified the chord progressions in "All Night, All Day."
- Students can play the chord progressions in "All Night, All Day" on keyboards, choirchimes, resonator bells, or Orff mallet instruments.
- Students have played or sung selections that have counter-melodies.

Procedures

1. Have students sing "All Night, All Day" while you play a chordal accompaniment.

2. Discuss with students other songs with countermelodies that they have played or sung. Help them identify what makes a good countermelody (for example, one in which the meter is the same as the melody; one in which the key is the same as that of the chord structure or chord progression used in the piece). List those characteristics on the chalkboard.

3. Have students work in small groups and take turns experimenting with improvising a countermelody on keyboards, choirchimes, resonator bells, or Orff mallet instruments, using only the pitches in the identified chords. Encourage students to make positive suggestions and to avoid critical remarks.

4. Have each group select one of the members to play his or her countermelody while they play the chordal accompaniment and the rest of the class sings the song.

5. After each performance, have students evaluate the countermelody using the list on the board to determine whether the countermelody displayed the special characteristics that they had identified.

Indicators of Success

- Students use keyboards, choirchimes, resonator bells, or Orff mallet instruments to improvise countermelodies for an entire piece.

Follow-up

- Have students explore different ways of playing chordal accompaniments—using arpeggios, tremolos, broken chords, and so on. Then have them experiment with two countermelodies, playing each along with the original melody of "All Night, All Day" and determining which combination gives the most pleasing overall effect.

STANDARD 3B

Improvising melodies, variations, and accompaniments: Students improvise melodic embellishments and simple rhythmic and melodic variations on given pentatonic melodies and melodies in major keys.

Objective

■ Students will improvise four-measure melodic variations on a given melodic phrase in a major key.

Materials

■ "In the Moonlight" ("Au Clair de la lune"), in *The Music Connection,* Grade 5 (Parsippany, NJ: Silver Burdett Ginn, 1995); *Share the Music,* Grade 3 (New York: Macmillan/McGraw-Hill, 1995); *Music and You,* Grade 3 (New York: Macmillan/McGraw-Hill, 1991); or *World of Music,* Grades 5 and 6 (Parsippany, NJ: Silver Burdett Ginn, 1991)

■ Xylophones

Prior Knowledge and Experiences

■ Students can play "In the Moonlight" in unison in a xylophone ensemble.

Procedures

1. Have the students, as an ensemble, play the melody of "In the Moonlight" on the xylophone. Guide students in analyzing the form of the song *(aaba).* Ask them to point out the four measures that make up the *b* phrase.

2. After students have identified the home tone and other pitches, have them make up new melodies for the *b* phrase, using only the original five notes (D, E, F#, G, and A) and keeping the same rhythm.

3. Have the complete ensemble play each occurrence of the *a* phrase and have volunteers take turns improvising the *b* phrase. Make sure each student has the opportunity to improvise on the *b* phrase.

4. Guide students in critiquing their improvisations and in analyzing the difficulties they may have had.

Indicators of Success

■ Students improvise four-measure melodic variations on the given phrase, maintaining the original rhythm and using the appropriate pitches.

Follow-up

■ Extend the activity by having students finalize an improvised phrase, notating their phrase to share with fellow players.

STANDARD 3C

Improvising melodies, variations, and accompaniments: Students improvise short melodies, unaccompanied and over given rhythmic accompaniments, each in a consistent style, meter, and tonality.

Objective

■ Students will improvise pentatonic melodies in various styles on the keyboard, accompanied by G♭ major and E♭ minor primary chords.

Materials

■ Keyboard synthesizers with built-in rhythms and one-finger chords

Prior Knowledge and Experiences

■ Students have explored the keyboard synthesizers and are familiar with the use of rhythm accompaniments and one-finger chord accompaniments.

■ Students have studied chord progressions on guitar or on a keyboard.

■ Students have sung ostinatos.

Procedures

1. Have students work in pairs at the keyboard, making up melodies using only the black keys. Tell the pairs that they may both play at the same time or take turns.

2. Ask students to select a style of rhythm that they like. Have the student sitting at the bass side play the chord accompaniment by finding the notes G♭, B (C♭), and D♭ (I, IV, and V chords in G♭ major) and making up a chord progression that repeats like an ostinato. Tell students to use one finger on the keys that are indicated. When the bass chord progression is secure, have the student on the treble side of the keyboard improvise a melody using any of the black keys.

3. Suggest the partners change places at the keyboard and continue their improvisations. Tell students to indicate when they are ready to play their improvisations for the class. Invite peer criticism. When you hear responses such as, "It sounds good (or bad)," "It doesn't sound together," and "The tune doesn't match the harmony," ask students to explain their comments. Lead students to discuss elements such as meter, tonality, and style with questions such as "Would one in a slow four be easier to work with?" or "What if you played the note G♭ more often in your melody?"

4. Change the chords that students may use to E♭, A♭, and B♭ and repeat the process, again using only black keys for the improvised melodies. Ask students to discuss how the change of chords affected the mood. Discuss major and minor tonality. (Some one-finger rhythmic harmonizations—especially rock style—on many synthesizers leave out the third, creating an open chord that may be interpreted as either major or minor. The E♭ minor, or *la* pentatonic, is similar to a blues scale with lowered third and seventh scale degrees; therefore, major, minor, or open fifth chords will fit the created melody.)

Indicators of Success

■ Students improvise pentatonic melodies in various styles on the keyboard, accompanied by G♭ major and E♭ minor primary chords.

Follow-up

- Review with students major and minor tonalities and relate chords and scales. For example, show how the primary chords are built from the C major scale.

- Play an accompaniment in E♭, G♭, C, or A minor on the sound system while the students improvise melodies on appropriate keys.

- Ask students to remember chord progressions and improvised melodies that they like so that they may share them with their classmates on another day.

Composing and arranging music within specified guidelines: Students will compose short pieces within specified guidelines, demonstrating how the elements of music are used to achieve unity and variety, tension and release, and balance.

Objective

- Students will compose and harmonize short melodic phrases.

Materials

- Chalkboard
- Manuscript paper

Prior Knowledge and Experiences

- Students can sing the major scale using solfège syllables.
- Students know that homophonic texture is made up of melody and chords.

Procedures

1. Notate a major scale on the board and explain that sometimes numbers are used to indicate scale degrees. Write numbers and solfège syllables under each pitch. Have students sing the scale, first with solfège syllables and then with numbers.

2. Explain to students that they can generate ideas for creating melodies by using ten-digit phone numbers; 1=*do*, 2=*re*, etc.; 8=*do*, 9=*re*, 0=*mi*. Do some examples together, having students sing each syllable as you point on the board to the numbers in each phone number. As some students discover that the melodies sound incomplete, discuss how each melody might be brought to completion by ending on a *do*. Play a phone number on the keyboard and have the students sing *do* as the last note.

3. Introduce the use of chords by showing how a chord may be built on *do*. Using that information, have the students build chords (writing them on the board and singing them) on the other scale tones. Write the Roman numeral designations under all of the chords.

4. Focus on the I, IV, and V chords and play them on the keyboard for the students. Explain the function of chords in a cadence and relate this to the discussion of ending melodies on *do*. Play several series of chords and have students indicate by hand signals which phrases sound complete and which sound incomplete.

5. Have students work as a class to harmonize a phone-number melody by adding chords (one chord per melody note). Explain that an easy way to get started is to be sure that the chord they use contains the melody note. Discuss choices; for example, if the note is *do*, they may choose the I, IV, or vi chord. After the piece is complete, play it on the keyboard for the class.

6. Have students write individual phone-number compositions with harmony. For example:

    1   4   1   4   5   5   5   4   9   1   7   1
    I IV I ii I   V   I IV V I   V   I

7. After students have completed their compositions, play several of them for the class.

Indicators of Success

- Students successfully create and harmonize melodies using specific chords to create a closing cadence in a major key.

Follow-up

- Extend the lesson by adding meter, rhythm, and individual playing on keyboards.

- Have students lengthen their compositions through variations on their melodies or by linking several melodies together.

Composing and arranging music within specified guidelines: Students will compose short pieces within specified guidelines, demonstrating how the elements of music are used to achieve unity and variety, tension and release, and balance.

Objective

- Students will create rondos using rhythm patterns based on their names.

Materials

- Two 4-by-6-inch cards for each student
- Rhythm instruments

Prior Knowledge and Experiences

- Students have performed and notated rhythms using the following values: whole note and rest, half note and rest, quarter note and rest, eighth note and rest.

- Students have listened to a rondo and analyzed the form.

Procedures

1. Have each student say his or her name several times, using a different rhythm pattern each time. Then have each student choose a favorite rhythm rendition of his or her name, notate it in large notes on one of the 4-by-6-inch cards, and print the name on the other card. Check students' notations by having them individually chant their names to you while you check their notation for accuracy.

Marikeesha Simpson

2. Assign students into groups of four (identifying Students A, B, C, and D in each group) to play three name games using their cards.

3. Game 1—"Chant." Have each group arrange their name cards in an order of their choice and establish a steady beat using patschen. Have them rhythmically chant the row of names they have set up without stopping, saying each name four times before moving on to the next name.

4. Game 2—"The Train." Again, have each group arrange their name cards in an order of their choice and establish a steady beat using patschen. Have Student A in each group chant his or her name in rhythm repeatedly. After the fourth repeat of Student A's name, have Student B enter and chant his or her name repeatedly. Have Students C and D enter and chant in turn in the same fashion, so that all four names will be chanted simultaneously.

5. Game 3—"The Rondo (ABACADA)." In each group, have each student chant his or her name four times in turn, creating a rondo by following the pattern ABACADA. Then have each student choose a rhythm instrument with which to reinforce his or her chant and repeat the rondo.

6. Have each group perform its rondo, using chants and instruments, for the rest of the class.

Indicators of Success

- Students accurately notate the rhythm patterns for their names.

- Students create compositions by arranging their names in an order of their choice.

- Students create rondos in ABACADA form and perform their rondos at a steady beat and with accurate rhythms.

Follow-up

- Have students add pitches to their rhythmic chants to create melodies.

STANDARD 4C

Composing and arranging music within specified guidelines: Students use a variety of traditional and nontraditional sound sources and electronic media when composing and arranging.

Objective

- Students will create compositions using alternative means of sound production to generate particular effects.

Materials

- Recording of "The Banshee," by Henry Cowell, in *The Music Connection,* Grade 2 (Parsippany, NJ: Silver Burdett Ginn, 1995); *Music and You,* Grade 3 (New York: Macmillan/McGraw-Hill, 1991); or *World of Music,* Grade 2 (Parsippany, NJ: Silver Burdett Ginn, 1991)

- Assortment of acoustic instruments

- Upright piano with front panels removed

- Audio-playback equipment

Prior Knowledge and Experiences

- Students have composed music using conventional instruments.

- Students have studied how a piano produces sound.

- Students have used nontraditional notation.

Procedures

1. Have the piano open so that the strings are visible when the students arrive. Ask students to suggest ways to produce sounds on the piano other than in the conventional manner, and demonstrate their suggestions. Explain that this is one way composers seek a wider selection of sounds to express their musical ideas.

2. Explain that in Gaelic folklore, a banshee is a female spirit whose wailing warns a family of an imminent death. Have students predict how a piece titled "The Banshee" might sound, and then play "The Banshee." Have students compare their predictions to what they heard.

3. Have students explore the acoustic instruments in the room, seeking different ways of producing sounds and seeing how many sounds they can generate. Ask each student to select one instrument and take a place in a circle on the floor to share his or her ideas.

4. Conduct the students in a sound improvisation. Point to individuals or groups and make motions that invite them to play, that ask them to stop, or that suggest dynamic levels, articulation, or tempo changes.

5. Invite students to become conductors, encouraging them to make up their own motions for getting the students to respond in certain ways.

6. Have students use nontraditional notation to help remember their created sounds. Explain that by putting together the various sounds in notation, the work becomes a composition.

7. Divide students into groups of three with their instruments. Have each group create a short composition using nontraditional sounds and notate their work using nontraditional notation. Then have groups play their compositions for the rest of the class.

Indicators of Success

- Students improvise on acoustic instruments using alternative sounds that they have discovered.
- Students use nontraditional notation to record their sounds and create compositions by putting the "sound notations" together.

Follow-up

- Have students listen again to "The Banshee" and then discuss the differences between composing and improvising.
- Invite students to write suggestions for another composition using nontraditional sounds including specific directions to students who will be interpreting the directions. Have students exchange compositions and practice what has been written by the other students. Invite students to perform for the composers, allowing the composers to evaluate the accuracy of the performance. Encourage the performers to evaluate the compositions for clarity in terms of notation and for interest.

Reading and notating music: Students read whole, half, quarter, eighth, sixteenth, and dotted notes and rests in 2/4, 3/4, 4/4, 6/8, 3/8, and alla breve meter signatures.

Objective

- Students will read nonpitched rhythm patterns consisting of whole, half, and quarter notes written in 4/4 meter.

Materials

- Guitar, keyboard, or other chordal instrument that can be used for accompaniment
- Teacher-generated rhythm sheets or transparency (see step 6)
- Overhead projector, if transparency is used
- Chalkboard

Prior Knowledge and Experiences

- None required.

Procedures

1. Play for students a progression of eight chords (for example, I, V, I, IV, I, IV, V, I) in any key as an accompaniment for keeping a steady beat. Play each chord for four counts, creating eight measures of accompaniment in 4/4 meter.

2. Have students stomp their feet once for each chord change:

   | | | |
   x

   Then have students snap their fingers twice for each chord change:

   | | | |
   x   x

   Finally, have students clap their hands four times for each chord change:

   | | | |
   x x x x

   Repeat until students are adept at the procedure.

3. Repeat step 2, changing the stomp to a sustained "buzz," the snaps to two sustained hums, and the claps to "ha's."

4. Without identifying the notes, show students on the chalkboard a whole note, a half note, and a quarter note. Then show students the words "whole note," "half note," and "quarter note" and ask them to match the words with the notes. Discuss which notes represent the stomp/buzz, the snap/hum, and the clap/ha.

5. Ask students to notate the stomp exercise on their own papers using whole notes. Give this exercise a name. Have students do the same with half notes for the snap exercise and with quarter notes for the clap exercise, and give each of these exercises a name. Have students practice the rhythms they have written.

6. Distribute rhythm sheets (or project the transparency) illustrating eight measures of whole, half, and quarter notes without mixing kinds of notes within measures. Have students clap these rhythms.

Indicators of Success

- Students accurately notate the rhythm patterns they have read.

- Keeping a steady beat, students accurately read rhythm patterns using quarter notes, half notes, and whole notes in 4/4 meter.

Follow-up

- Have students create and notate their own rhythm patterns using whole, half, and quarter notes. Illustrate them in large formats by having some students write them on the chalkboard or on poster board that can be mounted on the walls, or by projecting them on a screen using an opaque projector. Then have students read rhythms that others have notated.

- To begin pitch reading, add scale tones to rhythms that students have created.

- Use the same procedure for reading and notating rhythms in 6/8, 3/8, and alla breve meter signatures.

Reading and notating music: Students read whole, half, quarter, eighth, sixteenth, and dotted notes and rests in 2/4, 3/4, 4/4, 6/8, 3/8, and alla breve meter signatures.

Objective

- Students will accurately read and perform patterns using dotted notes.

Materials

- Transparency of "It's a Small World," "Ode to Joy," or "America the Beautiful"
- Overhead projector
- Chalkboard

Prior Knowledge and Experiences

- Students have learned to sing the selected song.
- Students have studied whole, half, quarter, eighth, and sixteenth notes.

Procedures

1. Draw a half note and a quarter note on the board and ask students to identify the notes.

2. Then add a dot after each note and ask students to guess what the value of the dot is for each note. If they say one beat for both, correct them by explaining that the dot adds one half the note's value.

3. Using the analogy of a "dotted dollar" being worth $1.50, have students then "dot" other items such as a gallon, their lunch period, their allowance, recess, a six-pack of soda, and so on.

4. Explain to students that because a quarter note has the same value as two eighth notes, a dotted quarter note would be worth a quarter note plus one eighth note (that is, half of a quarter note). Write the following example on the board, explaining each pattern as you notate it.

5. To check their understanding, ask individual students to clap a dotted quarter note–eighth note pattern. While most of the class maintains a steady clapping pattern, ask small groups or rows of students to perform clapping patterns in 4/4 meter that include the dotted quarter–eighth note pattern.

6. Have students sing the selected song and ask them to raise their hands when they hear the dotted quarter–eighth note pattern. Show the transparency of the song on the overhead projector to confirm their identification of the pattern.

Indicators of Success

■ Students accurately clap the dotted quarter–eighth note patterns.

■ Students accurately perform the dotted quarter–eighth note pattern in the selected song.

Follow-up

■ In their texts, have students find other pieces using dotted quarter notes and then perform the rhythms accurately.

Reading and notating music: Students read at sight simple melodies in both the treble and bass clefs.

Objective

- Students will correctly sing and play at sight two simple Baroque melodies.

Materials

- Two melodies from *Canon in D* by Johann Pachelbel (see step 2)
- Chalkboard or transparency
- Overhead projector, if transparency is used
- Recording of Pachelbel's *Canon in D*, in *The Music Connection*, Grade 8 (Parsippany, NJ: Silver Burdett Ginn, 1995); or *Music and You*, Grades 7 and 8 (New York: Macmillan/McGraw-Hill, 1991)
- Choirchimes, melody bells, or Orff mallet instruments
- Audio-playback equipment

Prior Knowledge and Experiences

- Students can sing the solfège syllables for the major scale.
- Given the location of *do,* students can label notes on the staff with solfège syllables.
- Students can read quarter-note rhythms.

Procedures

1. Ask students to look at the excerpts from Pachelbel's *Canon in D* and determine the solfège syllables for the notes.

2. As you point to the notes, have students sing Melody 1 using solfège syllables. Then do the same for Melody 2. Divide the class in half, assigning half to Melody 1 and half to Melody 2, and perform both parts together.

3. Invite individual students to play choirchimes, melody bells, or an Orff instrument, doubling the singing parts.

4. Explain that these melodies come from Pachelbel's *Canon in D,* which was composed during the Baroque period (1600–1750), when the popular style was ornate. Explain that one way composers made the music sound ornate was by layering melodies, giving the music a *polyphonic texture.*

5. Play a recording of the entire *Canon in D.* Have students raise their hands at each occurrence of one of the melodies they have been singing.

Indicators of Success

- Students correctly sing and play the two notated melodies.
- Students correctly indicate occurrences of these melodies in the *Canon in D.*

Follow-up

- Provide the students with notation or contour drawings of some of the other melodies in the *Canon in D* and have them identify them as they listen to the work. Have them read and sing the bass line to enhance another performance.

STANDARD 5C

Reading and notating music: Students identify and define standard notation symbols for pitch, rhythm, dynamics, tempo, articulation, and expression.

Objective

- Students will identify and define dynamic and tempo symbols.

Materials

- Handouts containing the poems "Sing a Song of People" (with expressive markings as in the accompanying figure) and "The Wind," in *Round About Six,* compiled by Margaret G. Rawlins (New York: F. Warne and Company, 1973)

Prior Knowledge and Experiences

- None required.

Procedures

1. Have students listen and follow on the handout while you read "Sing a Song of People," following designated dynamic and tempo symbols.

mf
Sing a song of people

rit.
Walking fast or slow

People in the city,

Up and down they go.

f
People on the sidewalk,

People in the bus;

Accel. - - - - - - - - - - -
People passing, passing,

- - - - - - - - - - - - - -
In back and front of us.

Excerpt from "Sing a Song of People" by Lois Lenski.

2. Read the poem aloud again, having students listen to discover and define the symbols used (*p, pp, mf, f, rit., accel., cresc., decresc.,* etc.).

3. Divide students into small groups and have them decide how to interpret the poem "The Wind." Have them place dynamic and tempo symbols above the appropriate words.

4. Have each group, or a representative from each group, read "The Wind," observing the dynamic and tempo symbols selected by the group. Check to see that students used correct symbols for their interpretation.

5. Since group interpretations will probably vary, discuss with the students how and why they differ.

6. Have groups exchange marked-up poems and ask groups, or individual students from each group, to read the poem, as marked, for the rest of the class. Invite the group that marked up each interpretation to critique the reading by others of their marked-up poem, determining whether the reading accurately reflected the dynamic and tempo symbols.

(continued)

Indicators of Success

- Students use correct dynamic and tempo symbols to reflect their interpretation of the poem "The Wind."
- Students correctly interpret dynamic and tempo symbols as they read each marked-up poem.

Follow-up

- Use a similar procedure with songs, demonstrating to students that both poetry and music have expressive qualities that should be purposefully performed to enhance the enjoyment of the art.

Reading and notating music: Students use standard notation to record their musical ideas and the musical ideas of others.

Objective

- Given a variety of rhythm patterns, students will notate, arrange, and perform a drum cadence of four phrases (sixteen measures).

Materials

- Pair of dice or a spinner for each group
- Manuscript paper
- Worksheet containing twelve possible rhythm patterns in 4/4 meter (see Rhythm Dicer Rhythms on page 40) for each group
- Instructions for the game (see step 1) for each group
- Audiocassette recorder with microphone and blank tape

Prior Knowledge and Experiences

- Students have clapped, chanted in rhythm syllables, and written rhythm patterns in 2/4, 3/4, and 4/4 meters.

Procedures

1. Read the class the instructions for the Rhythm Dicer game, a variation of Wolfgang Amadeus Mozart's musical dice game, "Musikalisches Würfelspiel."

   Rhythm Dicer Instructions

   The object of the game is to create and notate randomly a sixteen-measure drum or rhythm cadence. After completion of the cadence, students in each group will select percussion instruments to create a rhythm ensemble and then practice and perform their piece for the class. Notate your score carefully so that each student in the group will be playing the same rhythms.

   a. After getting together with your group, toss the dice. Let's say that the dice add up to 6.

   b. Find measure 6 on the Rhythm Dicer Rhythms sheet and copy it onto the first measure of your blank manuscript page.

   c. Toss the dice for the second measure of music. Let's say the dice add up to 12.

   d. Find measure 12 on the Rhythm Dicer Rhythms sheet and copy it onto the second measure of your manuscript page.

   e. Complete line one of your rhythm cadence by repeating this process for two more measures; complete line two by repeating this process for the next four measures.

   f. For line three, copy line one so that lines one and three are exactly the same; for line four, copy line two so that lines two and four are exactly the same.

   g. Practice clapping your completed rhythm cadence.

2. Divide the class into groups of four or five students. Give each group a set of game instructions, a worksheet, manuscript paper, and a pair of dice (or a spinner).

3. Have students follow Rhythm Dicer Instructions to create a sixteen-measure drum cadence.

4. After students have notated the sixteen measures consisting of four phrases, have them select percussion instruments to practice and perform their piece for other class members. Tape record their performances for future discussions.

(continued)

Indicators of Success

- Students accurately notate a sixteen-measure drum cadence.

- Students successfully read and perform their cadences.

Follow-up

- Using the recordings from step 4, have students critique each other's performances.

- Give students manuscript paper with the C major scale notated on the staff and labeled with letter names. Then give each group a xylophone or keyboard and invite them to add pitches to their rhythms, notate the melodies, and perform them.

Rhythm Dicer Rhythms

Reading and notating music: Students use standard notation to record their musical ideas and the musical ideas of others.

Objective

- Students will create and notate a twelve-tone composition.

Materials

- Transparency of excerpt from String Quartet no. 4, first movement, by Arnold Schoenberg, in *World of Music,* Grade 8 (Parsippany, NJ: Silver Burdett Ginn, 1991)
- Overhead projector
- Several sets of resonator bells
- Manuscript paper

Prior Knowledge and Experiences

- Students have studied major, minor, and whole-tone scales.
- Students have studied melodic and rhythmic notation.

Procedures

1. Demonstrate a chromatic scale on resonator bells. Show students how to write each note of the scale on the staff and discuss the functions of sharps, flats, and natural signs.

2. Have students discover how many different tones are in the scale. Discuss how some tones have the same sound but are called by two different names and are symbolized in two different ways on the staff (for example, F# and G♭).

3. Have students look at the example from the first movement of Schoenberg's String Quartet no. 4 to discover how the composer used the twelve tones of the chromatic scale to create a twelve-tone row. Note how he used all twelve tones before he repeated any.

4. Have students perform the Schoenberg twelve-tone row on resonator bells, playing it forward and backward.

5. Have students work in small groups to rearrange the resonator bells to create their own twelve-tone row. Explain that they may use whole notes for their first composition. Encourage groups to use the row in its original form (playing tones in order) and in retrograde form (playing it backward).

6. Have students notate their compositions on manuscript paper and perform them in their groups for the rest of the class.

Indicators of Success

- Students accurately notate and perform the twelve-tone row that they have created.

Follow-up

- Have students experiment with the rhythm of their twelve-tone compositions to make them more interesting. Then have them notate and perform their best efforts.

Listening to, analyzing, and describing music: Students describe specific music events in a given aural example, using appropriate terminology.

Objective

■ Students will identify an ostinato and explain how it contributes to a composition's unity.

Materials

■ Recording of "Unsquare Dance," by Dave Brubeck, in *The Music Connection,* Grade 7 (Parsippany, NJ: Silver Burdett Ginn, 1995); *Music and You,* Grade 8 (New York: Macmillan/McGraw-Hill, 1991); or *World of Music,* Grade 7 (Parsippany, NJ: Silver Burdett Ginn, 1991)

■ Audio-playback equipment

■ Chalkboard

Prior Knowledge and Experiences

■ Students have read and performed simple rhythm patterns.

■ From recorded examples, students have identified rhythm patterns that they have performed.

Procedures

1. Write the numbers 1 through 6 on the chalkboard horizontally. While softly counting the numbers, write x's under beats 1, 3, and 5 as follows:

Pattern 1: 1 2 3 4 5 6
           x   x   x

Establish a steady beat and have students count the beats, clapping the beats where the x's occur. Write the numbers 1 through 6 again, but this time write x's under beats 2, 4, and 6 as follows:

Pattern 2: 1 2 3 4 5 6
             x   x   x

Have students count the beats at a steady beat, again clapping the beats where the x's occur.

2. Add beats 7 and 8, extending the pattern, and add an x for clapping on beat 7 in Pattern 2. Have students practice both examples as follows:

Pattern 1: 1 2 3 4 5 6 7 8
           x   x   x

Pattern 2: 1 2 3 4 5 6 7 8
             x   x   x x

3. Erase beat 8, leaving a seven-beat pattern for both examples.

Pattern 1: 1 2 3 4 5 6 7
           x   x   x

Pattern 2: 1 2 3 4 5 6 7
             x   x   x x

4. Have students practice clapping or patching each pattern separately and then together, teacher versus class and then class divided into two groups.

5. Play the recording of "Unsquare Dance." Ask the class to find similarities and differences between the recording and the two patterns performed by the class. Help students to discover that both patterns are found in the piece, with Pattern 2 clapped. Note that the bass plays Pattern 1 with piano and sticks added.

6. Elicit how Pattern 1 continues throughout the piece. Explain that this repetitive pattern is an ostinato and that it unifies the composition.

7. Play the recording again and have students clap the ostinato (Pattern 1) throughout the composition, listening for how it provides unity through repetition.

Indicators of Success

- Students identify aurally both patterns on the recording.

- Students explain how an ostinato unifies "Unsqare Dance."

Follow-up

- Have students listen to other musical examples, with and without ostinatos. Ask them to identify which pieces have ostinatos.

- Teach the song "Garifalia" (also in 7/8 meter), in *Share the Music,* Grade 6 (New York: Macmillan/McGraw-Hill, 1995). Ask students questions such as the following: Does "Garifalia" have the same meter as "Unsquare Dance" or a different meter? Are the strong beats the same in each piece? Are the styles similar or different? Have students do a Venn diagram (see the example below) comparison of the two works, writing characteristics of "Unsquare Dance" in the left circle and characteristics of "Garifalia" in the right circle, and then writing the common features of the two pieces in the intersection of the two circles.

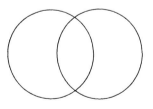

Venn diagram.

Listening to, analyzing, and describing music: Students describe specific music events in a given aural example, using appropriate terminology.

Objective

- Students will list five musical terms or phrases that describe an aural example.

Materials

- Three–four minute listening examples (different example for each group)
- Lists of musical terms or phrases (one copy for each group)
- Sheet of chart paper and a marker for each group
- Audio-playback equipment for each group

Prior Knowledge and Experiences

- Students have listened to various styles of music.
- Students have used descriptive terms (both musical and nonmusical) to evoke images and accurately reflect the music to which they have listened.

Procedures

1. Divide students into groups of four members each. Give each group a recorded listening example, a list of musical terms or phrases, chart paper and a marker, and audio-playback equipment. Review the terms to ensure that students know what they mean.

2. Direct each group to listen to its recording at least twice and then agree on five descriptive words or phrases (from the list provided) that accurately reflect what they have heard. Have the group incorporate these into a descriptive paragraph about the music. Then have one student from each group write the group's description on the chart paper.

3. Hang the chart papers with the descriptions so that they can all be seen. Play the recordings in random order and have students work within their groups to match the music examples with the descriptions on the chart papers. Award points to the groups that score well in matching descriptions to appropriate musical examples and to the group whose description is most often matched with the correct recording.

4. Play the recordings once again, having each group justify the musical terms used in its description. Have the class vote on which group had the most helpful, accurate description, and award extra points to that group.

5. Post the list of musical terms in a visible place in the room and encourage the class to use the terms when discussing music.

Indicators of Success

- Students demonstrate an increased ability to verbally describe listening examples using musical terms or phrases.

Follow-up

- To broaden the students' music vocabulary, give each group of students a music dictionary and ask them to select three different terms that could be used to describe another group's listening example. Have a student from each group write the group's terms on chart paper and, without identifying the selection described, share them with the other groups. Challenge the groups to match each new list of terms with the recording being described.

Listening to, analyzing, and describing music: Students describe specific music events in a given aural example, using appropriate terminology.

Objective

■ Students will identify and describe the variations of a theme in a classical selection.

Materials

■ "Simple Gifts," in *The Music Connection*, Grade 8 (Parsippany, NJ: Silver Burdett Ginn, 1995); *Share the Music*, Grade 5 (New York: Macmillan/McGraw-Hill, 1995); *Music and You*, Grades 5 and 7 (New York: Macmillan/McGraw-Hill, 1991); or *World of Music*, Grade 8 (Parsippany, NJ: Silver Burdett Ginn, 1991)

■ Recording of "Variations on Simple Gifts," from Aaron Copland's *Appalachian Spring*, in *The Music Connection*, Grade 8; or *Music and You*, Grade 5

■ Two or more guitars tuned to the chords of the song (i.e., at least one guitar tuned so that the tonic chord can be strummed on the open strings, and at least one guitar tuned so that the dominant chord can be strummed on the open strings)

■ Audio-playback equipment

Procedures

1. Have students sing the song "Simple Gifts." Call attention to the relative simplicity of the rhythm and the two-chord harmony, helping students to see that these contribute to the idea of simplicity that the text communicates.

2. Ask students to notice when they sing the song again what kind of mood it seems to convey. Have students join you in singing the song again while you accompany on the keyboard. Discuss the mood of the piece with the students.

3. Invite two or more students to accompany on guitars while the class sings the song again. Discuss how the addition of guitar affects the mood of the song.

4. Inform the students that Aaron Copland was a twentieth-century American composer who often used American folk melodies in his compositions. Explain that he used "Simple Gifts" as the theme in his ballet music for *Appalachian Spring*, and then created variations on this theme. Discuss the term "variations" and brainstorm with the class some ways Copland could vary the theme (for example, using different instruments and changing the rhythms).

5. Have students listen to the recording of the "Simple Gifts" theme and variations and raise their hands each time they hear a new variation begin. Ask them to keep track of the number of variations they hear.

6. Have students listen again and write a brief description of each variation in musical terms. After listening, discuss the students' answers with them.

Indicators of Success

■ Students describe the variations of "Simple Gifts" in musical terms.

(continued)

Prior Knowledge and Experiences

- Students can identify the instruments of the orchestra.
- Students have sung American folk songs.

Follow-up

- Using similar procedures, have students listen to other examples of theme and variations, such as Lucien Caillet's "Variations on the Theme 'Pop Goes the Weasel'," in *Share the Music,* Grade 3, or *Music and You,* Grade 4; or Charles Ives' *Variations on "America,"* in *The Music Connection,* Grades 4 and 6, *Share the Music,* Grade 4, *Music and You,* Grade 8, or *World of Music,* Grades 4 and 6. Have students compare how Copland and either Caillet or Ives created the variations.

STANDARD 6B

Listening to, analyzing, and describing music: Students analyze the uses of elements of music in aural examples representing diverse genres and cultures.

Objective

- Students will identify aurally how elements of music are used to modify a theme and create an introduction and bridges resulting in a theme and variations form.

Materials

- "When Johnny Comes Marching Home," in *The Music Connection*, Grades 5 and 8 (Parsippany, NJ: Silver Burdett Ginn, 1995); *Share the Music: Songs to Sing and Read* (New York: Macmillan/ McGraw-Hill, 1995); *Music and You*, Grade 7 (New York: Macmillan/McGraw-Hill, 1991); or *World of Music*, Grades 5, 6, and 8 (Parsippany, NJ: Silver Burdett Ginn, 1991)

- Recording of Morton Gould's "American Salute," in *The Music Connection*, Grade 5; *Share the Music*, Grade 6; or *Music and You*, Grade 7

- Clock with a second hand

- Worksheets containing only the numbers 1–12 (see step 5)

- Audio-playback equipment

- Chalkboard

Procedures

1. Have students sing "When Johnny Comes Marching Home" and clap its melodic rhythm. As students perform the song again, time their performance (about 20 seconds).

2. Tell the class that you will play another musical example that uses this song and that lasts approximately four minutes. Have students suggest ways the composer might have extended the piece, helping them to see that simple repetition will not maintain interest. Encourage students to consider what elements of music the composer might have used to extend it. Write student responses on the board.

3. Write the numbers 1–5 on the chalkboard. Have students listen to sections one through five of "American Salute." While students listen, point to numbers on the board as the various sections are played. Elicit ideas from students on what they heard.

4. Discuss with students how "American Salute" is based on one melody, called "A." Play sections one through five again and ask students how these sections might be labeled with letter names. Also, introduce terms such as introduction, coda, and bridge.

5. Distribute worksheets with the numbers 1–12 written horizontally, and have students listen to the recording and fill in their worksheets as you call out each number. Have students compare answers and agree upon the final version:

1	2	3	4	5	6	7	8	9	10	11	12
(Intro)	A	bridge	A1	A2	bridge	A3	bridge	A4	bridge	A5	coda

6. Invite individual students to describe how the elements of music were used to create the five variations (numbers 4, 5, 7, 9, and 11).

Indicators of Success

- Students demonstrate knowledge of the elements of music by suggesting ways that thematic material can be varied.

(continued)

Prior Knowledge and Experiences

■ Students have listened to and can identify repeating and contrasting sections in music using labels "A," "B," and so on.

■ Students have listened to and analyzed music in terms of music elements such as tone color, tempo, and dynamics.

■ Students successfully indicate the sections of the theme and variations and describe how they are different from each other.

Follow-up

■ Have students identify the theme and variations form in examples such as the second movement of Joseph Haydn's Symphony no. 94 in G, or Reinhold Glière's "Russian Sailor's Dance."

STANDARD 6C

Listening to, analyzing, and describing music: Students demonstrate knowledge of the basic principles of meter, rhythm, tonality, intervals, chords, and harmonic progressions in their analyses of music.

Objective

- Students will perform the I, IV, and V7 chords in a major key and explain the relationship of chords to the scale.

Materials

- Recording of "Dooji-Wooji," by Duke Ellington, in *The Music Connection,* Grade 7 (Parsippany, NJ: Silver Burdett Ginn, 1995); or *World of Music,* Grade 7 (Parsippany, NJ: Silver Burdett Ginn, 1991)
- Resonator bells
- Chalkboard

Prior Knowledge and Experiences

- Students can play resonator bells keeping a steady beat.
- Students can play harmonic accompaniments to songs.

Procedures

1. Distribute resonator bells for the G major scale and write the letter names of the notes in the G major chord on the chalkboard. Ask students with those bells (G, B, and D) to play a steady-beat accompaniment with the recording of "Dooji-Wooji" while the rest of the class raises their hands as soon as those bells do not fit the music (measure 5).

2. Write the letter names of the notes in the C major chord on the chalkboard and repeat step 1 (through measure 8) using the G and C chords, again having students determine by ear which chord of the two chords is correct for each measure.

   Harmonization for measures 1–8:

1	2	3	4	5	6	7	8
G	G	G	G	C	C	G	G

3. Write the letter names of the notes in the D7 chord on the board and have students play the G, C, D7 chord progression to a complete verse or more of "Dooji Wooji." The complete harmonization of "Dooji Wooji" is:

1	2	3	4	5	6	7	8	9	10	11	12
G	G	G	G	C	C	G	G	D7	D7	G	G

4. Ask students to determine which scale degrees (by numbers) are used for the three chords and then label the chords with Roman numerals. Note that this chord progression is called the 12-bar blues form.

I	I	I	I
IV	IV	I	I
V7	V7	I	I

5. Write the letter names of the notes in the G major scale on the board and explain how the notes of a scale provide the chord tones. Discuss the "every other letter" idea for chord building. Conclude with relating the I, IV, and V7 chords to the scale degrees.

(continued)

Indicators of Success

■ Students perform the I, IV, and V7 chords in a major key and accompany the recording using the twelve-bar progression.

Follow-up

■ Introduce "Going Back to Birmingham," in *The Music Connection,* Grade 7, as a blues song. Have students try accompanying it with the bells for the G major I, IV, and V7 chords played in the blues progression. Because the song is in F major, the students will hear that the G major chords do not fit. Write the F major scale on the board and help students construct the F, B♭, and C7 chords to accompany the song. Refer to the scale degrees for the I, IV, and V7 chords.

STANDARD 7A

Evaluating music and music performances: Students develop criteria for evaluating the quality and effectiveness of music performances and compositions and apply the criteria in their personal listening and performing.

Objective

- Students will develop criteria for evaluating music and musical performances and then use them to select compositions and performances for use in a mock radio station.

Materials

- Recordings of a variety of classical and jazz excerpts (about a dozen of each), including good-quality recordings, old scratchy recordings, and recordings of rehearsals
- Audio-playback equipment, including two audiocassette recorders
- Two blank audiocassettes

Prior Knowledge and Experiences

- Students have studied various musical styles and origins.
- Students have discussed their music preferences.
- Students have studied the elements of music.
- Students have written personal evaluations of music, using appropriate music vocabulary.

Procedures

1. Discuss with students the differences among radio stations that play music (for example, rock 'n' roll, classical, country, jazz). Ask them to give examples of the music played on a classical radio station versus that played on a jazz radio station (for example, music by Mozart, blues).

2. Discuss why some music is played on the air while other music is not (demographics of the audience, advertising revenues, ratings, and so on). Students might think about the stations they normally listen to and transfer that knowledge to classical and jazz stations.

3. Ask students to create a list of criteria for what makes an effective musical performance and what makes a good piece of music. Discuss with them the importance of all performers playing together with good balance, blend, and so on, and the significance of music having repetition and contrast for unity and variety, and so on.

4. Divide the class in half and assign one of the groups to be employees of a classical radio station and the other group to be employees of a jazz radio station. Then assign half of each group to be salespeople and the other half to be program directors or disc jockeys. Explain the roles of people in these positions at radio stations.

5. Have students in each group—classical and jazz—listen to the respective recordings of excerpts and then select music that meets their requirements. Have each group of salespeople compile a list of six songs to present to their program director group for air play with a list of reasons for including those pieces.

6. Have the program directors listen to the recordings, read the reasons, and select for their station three songs (a set) and the order in which they should be played. Then have the disc jockeys make a cassette recording of their set, including an appropriate introduction for each song, giving the performer, the type of composition, and some background, if appropriate.

7. Play the two sets for the entire class and have students decide whether the sets played for each of the stations meet the criteria they originally devised.

(continued)

Indicators of Success

- Students create criteria for evaluating music and performances and apply them to specific musical selections.

- Students use music terminology (verbally and in writing) accurately to describe the music they consider to be of good quality.

Follow-up

- Have students decide what music they will perform in a concert based on criteria they have established for the performance. Then have them write the program and program notes for the concert.

STANDARD 8A

Understanding relationships between music, the other arts, and disciplines outside the arts:
Students compare in two or more arts how the characteristic materials of each art can be used to transform similar events, scenes, emotions, or ideas into works of art.

Objective

- Students will compare telling a story through the art of music in an opera to telling the same story through the art of theatre in a play, identifying the unique characteristics of opera that help enrich such story telling.

Materials

- Synopsis of one scene of a well-known opera, such as *Carmen, The Barber of Seville,* or *Gianni Schicchi*
- Recording of the music for the selected opera scene
- Audio-playback equipment
- Chalkboard or blank transparency
- Overhead projector, if transparency is used

Prior Knowledge and Experiences

- Students have engaged in improvisatory activities.

Procedures

1. Ask students to name different ways to tell a story and list these ideas on the chalkboard or on a transparency.

2. If students do not offer the idea of opera, ask, "Who can tell me what we call a work of music that tells a story through singing?" Discuss similarities and differences between operas and musicals or between those forms and other responses that are given.

3. Distribute the synopsis of a scene from the selected opera. Encourage a discussion of the story at that point in the opera. Then select a group of students to improvise the story.

4. After the students' improvised dramatization of the story, play the recording from that scene in the opera. Have the students identify ways in which the music enhances the telling of the story.

5. Ask them to compare the opera performance with their improvised dramatization, identifying similarities and differences. Through questioning, guide the students to see how each version has dimensions not present in the others.

Indicators of Success

- Students identify similarities and differences between telling the selected story through opera versus through theatre without music.

Follow-up

- Discuss with students how the visual arts enhance the telling of a story. Have them identify ways in which the visual arts would enhance the opera scene that they have been studying.

Understanding music in relation to history and culture: Students describe distinguishing characteristics of representative music genres and styles from a variety of cultures.

Objective

- Students will identify the distinguishing characteristics (for example, instruments, timbres, and textures) of representative music genres and styles from a variety of cultures.

Materials

- Microsoft's *Musical Instruments* CD-ROM (for Macintosh or IBM-compatible computers)

- Several computers with CD-ROM capabilities (one for each group)

Prior Knowledge and Experiences

- Students have worked with CD-ROM.

Procedures

1. Introduce the class to the *Musical Instruments* software. Demonstrate how they can access information on instruments by family, geographic area of origin, ensemble in which they might be found, and alphabetically. Also, demonstrate how they can hear the sounds of the various instruments.

2. Assign groups of students to begin to explore, using the software, similar types of instruments from different cultures (e.g., "bagpipes of Continental Europe, Asia, and Great Britain," or "drums of Southeast Asia, Africa, North America, and Europe," or "instruments of the gamelan, the Baroque orchestra, the jazz combo, and the koto orchestra").

3. Have students look for similarities and differences among the instruments in uses, timbre, construction material, and so on. Move from group to group to assist students in using the software.

4. Have students from each group give a brief description of their findings to the class by playing a representative music example from their assigned culture and describing identifying characteristics.

Indicators of Success

- Students identify and describe distinguishing characteristics of representative music examples from a variety of cultures.

- Students describe characteristics of instruments, ensembles, and music genres and styles from cultures they have researched.

Follow-up

- Working with the geography or history teacher, have students explore the impact of the availability of resources or of significant events upon music making in several of the cultures researched in the music class.

Understanding music in relation to history and culture: Students describe distinguishing characteristics of representative music genres and styles from a variety of cultures.

Objective

- Students will describe the special characteristics of the habanera and perform on classroom instruments in the style of a habanera using its characteristic rhythms.

Materials

- "Habanera," from *Carmen,* by Georges Bizet, with accompanying recording, in *World of Music,* Grade 8 (Parsippany, NJ: Silver Burdett Ginn, 1991)
- Finger cymbals, woodblocks, castanets, and tambourines
- Opaque projector
- Audio-playback equipment

Prior Knowledge and Experiences

- Students can clap subdivided beats.
- Students have sung, played, or listened to Spanish music.

Procedures

1. Briefly tell the class the story of the opera *Carmen* without telling students the locale for the opera. Explain that for Carmen, freedom is the most important thing, exemplified in "Habanera," which she sings early in Act I of the opera.

2. Put the following rhythm patterns on the board:

Have students clap the rhythm patterns. If the class is not skilled in reading rhythmic notation, use mnemonic devices to reinforce the patterns (for example, "Escamillo" for the first rhythm pattern; "opera" on the triplets, "Carmen" on the eighth notes, for the second rhythm pattern).

3. When students can clap the rhythms accurately, explain that the habanera is a dance in which the performers move in a stately manner. Have the class move to the beat in such a manner and clap the rhythms with their hands above their heads.

4. Give some students rhythm instruments (such as finger cymbals, woodblocks, castanets, and tambourines) to play the various rhythm patterns.

5. Play "Habanera" from *Carmen* for the class. Have students listen for the rhythms they have just practiced and be prepared to describe what they hear. Play "Habanera" again, asking students to listen for the percussion instruments Bizet used to orchestrate this piece. Discuss with the class how the instruments used give the music its special characteristics.

6. Ask students what country they think is the location for the opera. Then ask whether the rhythms or the percussion instruments used remind them of the Spanish music they are familiar with, and if so, in what way. Explain that the habanera was developed in Cuba and that it was named after the capital, Havana. Tell students that the dance became popular all over Europe, especially in Spain.

(continued)

Indicators of Success

- Students identify and describe the special characteristics of the habanera.

- Students perform the characteristic rhythms of the habanera on classroom percussion instruments.

Follow-up

- Divide the class into small groups and have them devise their own version of the habanera to perform for each other. Ask them to describe how their version compares with the characteristic habanera.

Understanding music in relation to history and culture: Students describe distinguishing characteristics of representative music genres and styles from a variety of cultures.

Objective

- Students will identify characteristics of gagaku, a form of Japanese court music.

Materials

- Recording of "Entenraku," in *The Music Connection*, Grade 6 (Parsippany, NJ: Silver Burdett Ginn, 1995); or from *Gagaku: Japanese Court Music*, Lyrichord 7126

- *100 Views of Edo: The Wave*, wood-block print by Ando Hiroshige, in *The Music Connection*, Grade 8

- Audio-playback equipment

Prior Knowledge and Experiences

- Students have studied the difference between homophonic and heterophonic music.

- Students have studied the basic axiom of Japanese art— "maximum effect from minimum material"—in relation to Japanese temples, shrines, woodcuts, and flower arrangements.

Procedures

1. Have students listen to the first section of "Entenraku," an example of gagaku (a form of Japanese court music), to decide whether the musical texture is thick or thin and how the texture compares with the economy of means practiced in the visual arts. Explain that the Japanese value each sound as a single thread in a fine tapestry; sounds are limited so that the listener can carefully follow each strand.

2. Have students listen again for the instrumental timbres that are used in "Entenraku." Help them list instruments and their timbres:

   Oboe *(hichirichi)*

   Mouth organ *(sho)*

   Strings (koto and *biwa)*

   Drums *(taiko* and *kakko)*

3. Have students review what heterophonic structure is: one melody is played and varied simultaneously as the melodic lines shift ahead and behind each other in a sliding-door effect. Ask whether they noted this structure in "Entenraku." Make sure students note that some instruments played only essential tones.

4. Explain to students that a "breath rhythm" in gagaku is a lengthening of the last beat of each measured unit. Breath rhythm is used not only in gagaku but also in noh and Kabuki theater music. It could be compared to a rubato or ritard in Western music. Have students conduct in 4/4, using a breath rhythm on the fourth beat. Explain that the breath rhythm creates great tension as it leads to the following beat, and that one of the thrills of gagaku is watching the drummer's hands rise high in the air as he anticipates that next beat.

5. Have students each select a "time-keeper" instrument to listen for and, while listening to the recording, play its pattern with their fingers on the desks, noting whether their instruments mark off beats or large sections. Note that the small drum *(kakko)* keeps the beat; the large drum *(taiko)* marks off larger sections; and the strings (koto and *biwa)* also perform percussive functions, with arpeggios marking larger sections. Melodic, interlocking ostinatos provide the basic time organization.

(continued)

6. Ask students to summarize what they have learned about gagaku music. List the special, defining characteristics on the board.

Indicators of Success

■ Students identify characteristics of gagaku music.

Follow-up

■ Have students compare gagaku music with Western orchestral music they have heard and discover similarities and differences.

STANDARD 9C

Understanding music in relation to history and culture: Students compare, in several cultures of the world, functions music serves, roles of musicians, and conditions under which music is typically performed.

Objective

- Students will compare roles and functions of music in Native American culture with those in Eastern European culture.

Materials

- "Go, My Son," in *The Music Connection,* Grade 6 (Parsippany, NJ: Silver Burdett Ginn, 1995); *Share the Music,* Grade 5 (New York: Macmillan/McGraw-Hill, 1995); or *World of Music,* Grade 6 (Parsippany, NJ: Silver Burdett Ginn, 1991)

- Audiocassette recording (with sign language) of "Whip Man," Wapato Indian Club, c/o Sue Rigdon, Wapato Middle School, Wapato, WA 98956

- Recording of *Music of Bulgaria,* Ensemble of the Bulgarian Republic, Philip Koutev, Warner Communications 972011-2

- Drum

Procedures

1. Demonstrate the sign language for "Go, My Son." Explain that sign language is not universal and can be different for different tribes or nations. [*Note:* If students have experience with any form of signing, they may make comparisons to the signing for "Go, My Son."]

2. Have students imitate your motions as you sing and sign the song. After a few repetitions, have students sing and sign the song from memory, adding an ostinato played on the drum in each measure:

$$\frac{4}{4} \quad \textJ. \quad \textJ \quad \textJ$$

3. Introduce "Whip Man," dimming the lights to create the atmosphere for this special piece. Explain that many Native Americans did not physically discipline their children but left that job to the "whip man," who went from tribe to tribe for that purpose. Perform the signing for "Whip Man" while playing the recording for the students. Teach them the entire story in sign language, first by speaking the words and then singing and signing along with the record.

4. Discuss the symbolism in the motions, reminding students that the piece is serious and that their posture and expression should reflect the dignity of the people who created it. Explain that among the functions of Native American music are teaching values to the public, setting trends, bringing awareness about issues, and preserving traditions.

5. Explain that in some cultures music can serve specific functions in daily living and that it can chronicle historic events. Play "Tamburi Drankat" ("The Drums Roll"), from *Music of Bulgaria,* and ask the students whom they think is singing this song. Explain that, while they sew, Bulgarian women sing songs that describe all aspects of life in their country. Tell them that "Tamburi Drankat" is a type of work song. Then ask them to suggest the type of work the music could be describing. (People going to harvest, crying out to one another across the fields.) Discuss the musical characteristics that create this impression.

(continued)

Prior Knowledge and Experiences

- Students have viewed the videocassette *The Dennis Alley Wisdom Dancers in Concert at the Grand Canyon* (PO Box 33053, Phoenix, AZ 85067; telephone 602-244-9903), including Alley's rendition of "Go, My Son."

- Students have been learning about the culture of various Native American Indian nations.

6. Have students compare the musical roles and functions of these two different examples of world cultures.

Indicators of Success

- Students describe the roles and functions of music in the two cultures and compare them to each other.

Follow-up

- Have students compare the vocal timbre and rhythmic and harmonic structures of the songs "Whip Man" and "Tamburi Drankat."

- Have students listen to examples of contemporary Native American music, such as *Reservation of Education,* by Robby Bee and the Boyz from the Rez (Sound of America Records, PO Box 8606, Albuquerque, NM 87198; telephone 505-268-6110), WAR 604. Have them compare its message about living to the message in songs of the past.

RESOURCES

Sources of Songs Used in This Text

Leck, Henry, and Prince Julius Adeniyi, arr. "Three Yoruba Native Songs of Nigeria." Fort Lauderdale, FL: Plymouth Music Company, 1994.

The Music Connection, Grades K–8. Parsippany, NJ: Silver Burdett Ginn, 1995.

Music and You, Grades K–8. New York: Macmillan/McGraw-Hill, 1991.

Share the Music, Grades K–6. New York: Macmillan/McGraw-Hill, 1995.

World of Music, Grades K–8. Parsippany, NJ: Silver Burdett Ginn, 1991.

Listening Selections Used in This Text

Bizet, Carmen. "Habanera," from *Carmen.*

Brubeck, Dave. "Unsquare Dance."

Caillet, Lucien. "Variations on the Theme 'Pop Goes the Weasel'."

Copland, Aaron. "Variations on Simple Gifts," from *Appalachian Spring.*

Cowell, Henry. "The Banshee."

Ellington, Duke. "Dooji-Wooji."

Gagaku: Japanese Court Music. Lyrichord, 7126.

Glière, Reinhold. "Russian Sailor's Dance."

Gould, Morton. "American Salute."

Haydn, Joseph. Symphony no. 94 in G.

Ives, Charles. *Variations on 'America.'*

Music of Bulgaria. Ensemble of the Bulgarian Republic. Philip Koutev. Warner Communications 972011-2.

Pachelbel, Johann. *Canon in D.*

Reservation of Education. Robby Bee and the Boyz from the Rez. WAR 604. Available from Sound of America Records, PO Box 8606, Albuquerque, NM 87198; telephone 505-268- 6110.

"Sakura."

Schoenberg, Arnold. String Quartet no. 4, first movement.

"Whip Man." Wapato Indian Club, c/o Sue Rigdon, Wapato Middle School, Wapato, WA 98956. Audiocassette.

Other Materials Used in This Text

The Dennis Alley Wisdom Dancers in Concert at the Grand Canyon. 1988. PO Box 33053, Phoenix, AZ 85067; telephone 602-244-9903. Videocassette.

Musical Instruments. Microsoft, Redmond, WA. CD-ROM.

Rawlins, Margaret G., compiler. *Round About Six.* New York: F. Warne and Company, 1973. Book of poetry.

Additional Resources

*Anderson, William M., and Patricia Shehan Campbell. *Multicultural Perspectives in Music Education.* 2d ed. Reston, VA: Music Educators National Conference, 1996.

Erdei, Peter, ed. *150 American Folk Songs to Sing, Read and Play.* New York: Boosey & Hawkes, 1974.

Feldstein, Sandy, ed. *The World's Greatest Songbook: A Collection of Over 250 of Your Favorite Songs.* Van Nuys, CA: Alfred Publishing Company, 1988.

Feldstein, Sandy, and Morton Manus. *It's Recorder Time Holiday Song Book.* Van Nuys, CA: Alfred Publishing Company, 1982.

Music Educators National Conference. *Get America Singing . . . Again!* Milwaukee: Hal Leonard Corporation, 1996.

*Available from MENC

MENC Resources on Music and Arts Education Standards

Implementing the Arts Education Standards. Set of five brochures: "What School Boards Can Do," "What School Administrators Can Do," "What State Education Agencies Can Do," "What Parents Can Do," "What the Arts Community Can Do." 1994. #4022. Each brochure is also available in packs of 20.

National Standards for Arts Education: What Every Young American Should Know and Be Able to Do in the Arts. 1994. #1605.

Opportunity-to-Learn Standards for Music Instruction: Grades PreK–12. 1994. #1619.

Performance Standards for Music: Strategies and Benchmarks for Assessing Progress Toward the National Standards, Grades PreK–12. 1996. #1633.

Perspectives on Implementation: Arts Education Standards for America's Students. 1994. #1622.

Prekindergarten Music Education Standards. Brochure. 1995. #4015 (set of 10).

The School Music Program—A New Vision: The K–12 National Standards, PreK Standards, and What They Mean to Music Educators. 1994. #1618.

Teaching Examples: Ideas for Music Educators. 1994. #1620.

MENC's *Strategies for Teaching* Series

Strategies for Teaching Prekindergarten Music, compiled and edited by Wendy L. Sims. #1644.

Strategies for Teaching K–4 General Music, compiled and edited by Sandra L. Stauffer and Jennifer Davidson. #1645.

Strategies for Teaching Middle-Level General Music, compiled and edited by June M. Hinckley and Suzanne M. Shull. #1646.

Strategies for Teaching High School General Music, compiled and edited by Keith P. Thompson and Gloria J. Kiester. #1647.

Strategies for Teaching Elementary and Middle-Level Chorus, compiled and edited by Ann Roberts Small and Judy Bowers. #1648.

Strategies for Teaching High School Chorus, compiled and edited by Randal Swiggum. #1649.

Strategies for Teaching Strings and Orchestra, out-of-print. Please view the online version at www.menc.org

Strategies for Teaching Middle-Level and High School Keyboard, compiled and edited by Martha F. Hilley and Tommie Pardue. #1655.

Strategies for Teaching Beginning and Intermediate Band, compiled and edited by Edward J. Kvet and Janet M. Tweed. #1650.

Strategies for Teaching High School Band, compiled and edited by Edward J. Kvet and John E. Williamson. #1651.

Strategies for Teaching Specialized Ensembles, compiled and edited by Robert A. Cutietta. #1653.

Strategies for Teaching Middle-Level and High School Guitar, compiled and edited by William E. Purse, James L. Jordan, and Nancy Marsters. #1654.

Strategies for Teaching: Guide for Music Methods Classes, compiled and edited by Louis O. Hall with Nancy R. Boone, John Grashel, and Rosemary C. Watkins. #1656.

Strategies for Teaching: Technology, compiled and edited by Sam Reese, Kimberly McCord, and Kimberly Walls. #1657.

For more information on these and other MENC publications, write to or call MENC Publications Sales, 1806 Robert Fulton Drive, Reston, VA 20191-4348; 800-828-0229.